what would you ask?
MARIE CURIE

Anita Ganeri
Illustrated by Liz Roberts

Thameside Press

Distributed in the United States by
Smart Apple Media
1980 Lookout Drive
Mankato, MN 56003

Text copyright © Anita Ganeri 2000

Printed in the USA

Editor: Veronica Ross
Designer: Caroline Grimshaw
Illustrator: Liz Roberts
Consultants: Hester Collicutt and Alison Porter

Library of Congress Cataloging-in-Publication Data

Ganeri, Anita, 1961-
    Marie Curie / by Anita Ganeri.
        p. cm. -- (What would you ask?)
    Includes index.
    Summary: A biography of the chemist whose work with radium laid the foundation
for much of today's scientific knowledge, told in the form of an imagined interview.
    ISBN 1-929298-09-9
    1. Curie, Marie, 1867-1934--Juvenile literature. 2. Chemists--Poland--Biography--
Juvenile literature. [1. Curie, Marie, 1867-1934. 2.
Chemists. 3. Women--Biography.] I. Title.

QD22.C8 G35 2000
540'.92--dc21
[B]   00-024745

9 8 7 6 5 4 3 2 1

Contents

What do you do?   4

Where were you born?   6

What were you like at school?   8

Did you always want to be a scientist?   10

Did you go to a college?   12

What did you do when you left?   14

What was your greatest discovery?   16

How did you discover radium?   18

What was your worst moment?   20

What makes you most proud?   22

How did radium change your life?   24

How is Marie Curie remembered today?   26

Some important dates   28

Glossary   30

Index   32

What do you do?

"I am a scientist. I was the first person to discover radium."

In 1898, Marie Curie discovered a brand-new chemical substance called radium. The discovery changed her life. It also changed the path of science.

Marie's work on radioactivity (the way in which radium and other substances give off powerful rays) helped scientists learn more about atoms and the enormous energy locked inside them.

Today, this energy is used to run nuclear power stations and in industry. Doctors also use the rays to treat diseases such as cancer.

Marie Curie became one of the most famous scientists in the world. But she had to struggle to prove her worth. In those days, many people did not believe that a woman could be a scientist. Marie showed that women are equal to men. She was the first woman in Europe to become a Doctor of Science and won two Nobel Prizes. Her story inspired many other women to follow in her footsteps.

Where were you born?

"I was born in Warsaw, Poland."

Marie was born on November 7, 1867 in Freta Street, Warsaw, in Poland. She was named Maria Salomee Sklodowska, though her family always called her Manya. Marie was the youngest of five children and had three sisters and a brother.

Marie's parents were teachers, and Marie was born in a school. This was a boarding school for girls where her mother was principal, and where the family lived with the pupils.

Marie adored her parents, even though they were strict.
She knew her mother loved her even though she
never hugged or kissed her. Mrs. Sklodowska
was ill with tuberculosis and did not want
to pass on her germs. She grew weak and
thin, and coughed-up blood which she
quickly hid in her handkerchief.
In 1876, Marie's sister Sofia fell ill
and died. Two years later, when
Marie was just 10 years old,
her mother also died.

What were you like at school?

"I loved school and worked hard at my studies."

It took Marie and her family a long time to recover from her mother's death. Without her, the house felt sad and empty, and Marie felt very lost and alone. To hide her feelings, she buried herself in her books. Marie learned to read and write when she was just five years old. Now she read everything she could—adventure stories, poetry, even her father's science books.

At school, Marie was a brilliant pupil. She took her
studies very seriously and worked very hard.
In 1883, she graduated from high school top of
her class, with a gold medal for outstanding
achievement. But Marie was worn out
from all her hard work, so her father
sent her to stay with relatives in
the country. She had a wonderful
time, going for sleigh rides
and picnics, and learning
how to row and ride.

Did you always want to be a scientist?

"I always liked science, but I planned to be a teacher."

With school behind them, Marie and her sisters had to find a way to earn their living. There were very few jobs for young people in Poland, so the sisters gave private lessons, for a small charge, to children from Warsaw families.

Marie and Bronya longed to be able to carry on studying. But Warsaw University did not take girls as students. Then Marie had a brilliant plan. With their savings, the two sisters would send Bronya to Paris to study medicine at the Sorbonne. When Bronya qualified as a doctor, she would send for Marie to join her.

Marie left Warsaw and took a job as a governess. She sent some of her wages to Bronya. Marie worked long hours, and although the family treated her well, she was often homesick. Any spare time she had was spent reading science books.

Did you go to a college?

"Yes. I went to a university called the Sorbonne in Paris."

In the fall of 1891, Marie boarded a train for Paris. She would live with Bronya and her new husband. To save money, she traveled cheaply in third class. She packed her own food for the three-day trip and took her own folding chair, as there weren't any seats! She hated leaving her father behind but promised that she would soon be back.

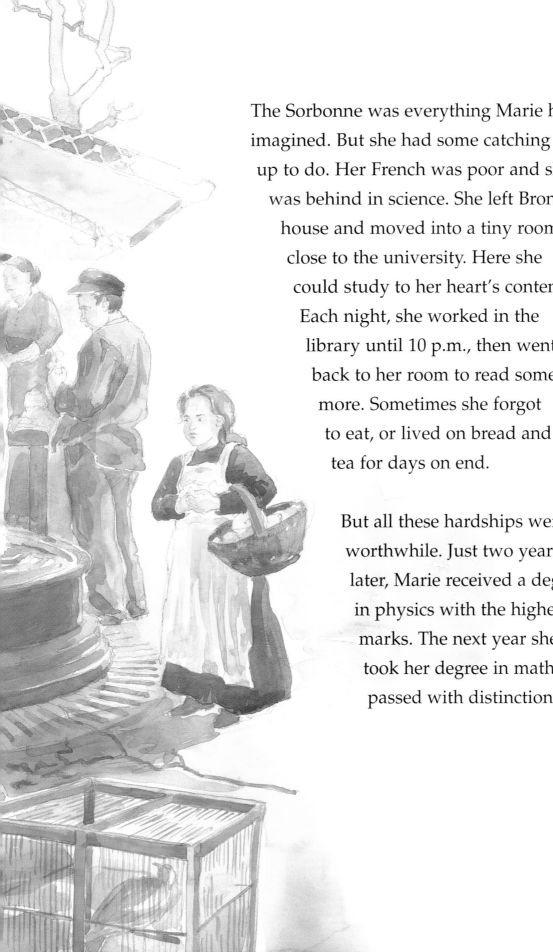

The Sorbonne was everything Marie had imagined. But she had some catching up to do. Her French was poor and she was behind in science. She left Bronya's house and moved into a tiny room close to the university. Here she could study to her heart's content. Each night, she worked in the library until 10 p.m., then went back to her room to read some more. Sometimes she forgot to eat, or lived on bread and tea for days on end.

But all these hardships were worthwhile. Just two years later, Marie received a degree in physics with the highest marks. The next year she took her degree in math and passed with distinction.

What did you do when you left?

"I married, and started working as a scientist."

Apart from finishing her degree, there was another reason why 1894 was an important year for Marie. She met and fell in love with Pierre Curie, a distinguished French scientist. Marie and Pierre were married on July 26, 1895. Maria Sklodowska was now Marie Curie! They spent their honeymoon cycling through the French countryside.

After their marriage, Marie went to work alongside Pierre at the School of Physics in Paris. She wanted to study for her Doctor of Science award. But first she had to find a subject for her thesis, or research paper. It had to be something new and original.

Marie began reading the latest work carried out by
scientists all over the world. One report caught her eye.
It was written by French scientist, Henri Becquerel.
A year earlier, a German scientist, Wilhelm Röntgen, had
discovered X-rays. He called them "X" because he did
not know what they were. While investigating
X-rays, Becquerel discovered that the metal
uranium also gave off mysterious rays.
Marie had found her subject. She would
research the mysterious rays.

What was your greatest discovery?

"Finding two brand-new chemicals, never seen before."

Marie was given a tiny room in the School of Physics as her laboratory. It was damp, drafty, and icy cold. But Marie did not mind. She quickly set to work.

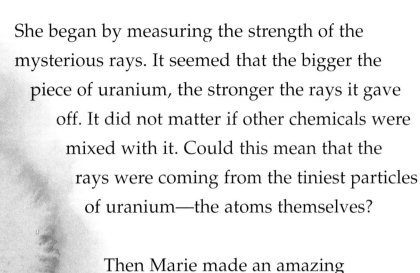

She began by measuring the strength of the mysterious rays. It seemed that the bigger the piece of uranium, the stronger the rays it gave off. It did not matter if other chemicals were mixed with it. Could this mean that the rays were coming from the tiniest particles of uranium—the atoms themselves?

Then Marie made an amazing discovery. She knew that a rock called pitchblende contained uranium. But, to her astonishment, the rays were four times stronger than they should have been. There was only one explanation: there must be another substance in the pitchblende that was giving off radiation.

Marie tested the pitchblende for every chemical she knew. But none of them gave off rays. That meant that the pitchblende must contain a brand-new chemical. But it was even more exciting than that. In fact, Marie and Pierre discovered not one but two new chemicals—polonium, named after Poland, and radium.

17

How did you discover radium?

"With a lot of very hard work!"

Some scientists did not believe Marie and Pierre. They wanted proof that radium was real. They asked the Curies to make a sample of pure radium. It was easier said than done!

Tons of pitchblende were needed to make the tiniest sample of radium. A factory supplied them with pitchblende, but where could they work? Marie's laboratory was much too small. They found a large, leaky shed behind the School of Physics, abandoned because no one else wanted to work there.

Marie and Pierre began sorting the pitchblende.
First they sifted it to remove any garbage. Then they
ground it, boiled it, and separated out the solids.
These were dissolved in acid and treated to
separate out the chemicals. It was back-breaking
work and the Curies were exhausted and often
ill. But they had to carry on.

Then, one winter's evening in 1902, came the
moment they had wanted. After almost four
years of work, Marie finally had her pure
radium. It was only 0.1 gram (0.035 ounce),
just a speck. But it was enough to show the world.

What was your worst moment?

"When Pierre was killed."

In June 1903, Marie received her Doctor of Science degree. In December came an even greater honor. Marie, Pierre, and Henri Becquerel were awarded the Nobel Prize for Physics for their work on radioactivity.

The following year, Pierre was appointed professor at the Sorbonne and Marie became his chief assistant. It was one of the happiest times of their lives. Then disaster struck. On April 19, 1906, Pierre was walking along a Paris street, deep in thought. Crossing the street, he stepped right in front of a horse-drawn wagon. He was killed instantly.

Marie was devastated by Pierre's death. Once again, she threw herself into her work. The university offered her Pierre's job and Marie became the Sorbonne's first woman professor. She began her first lecture at exactly the place where Pierre had finished. In 1911, at the age of 44, Marie won the Nobel Prize for chemistry. She was the first person to win two Nobel Prizes.

What makes you most proud?

"Probably the Radium
Institute in Paris!"

Marie traveled to Stockholm in Sweden
to collect her second Nobel Prize, but
afterwards she fell ill. She went to stay
with her friend, Hertha Ayrton, in
England until she recovered.

When she returned to Paris in 1912,
the famous Pasteur Institute made
her an offer she could not refuse.
For years, she had dreamed of
having a laboratory devoted to the
study of radioactivity. This was
what Pierre would have wanted.
Now she was offered a new
laboratory on the newly-named
Rue Pierre Curie. Half of the
building was for research.
The other half was for the
medical uses of radiation,
especially for treating cancer.
By 1914, the Radium Institute
was finished.

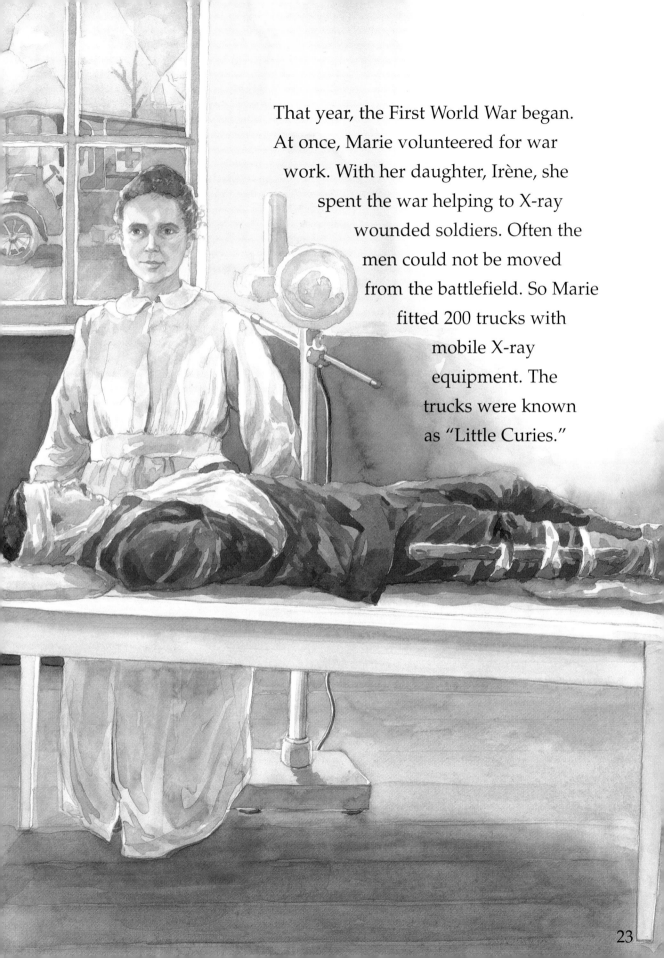

That year, the First World War began. At once, Marie volunteered for war work. With her daughter, Irène, she spent the war helping to X-ray wounded soldiers. Often the men could not be moved from the battlefield. So Marie fitted 200 trucks with mobile X-ray equipment. The trucks were known as "Little Curies."

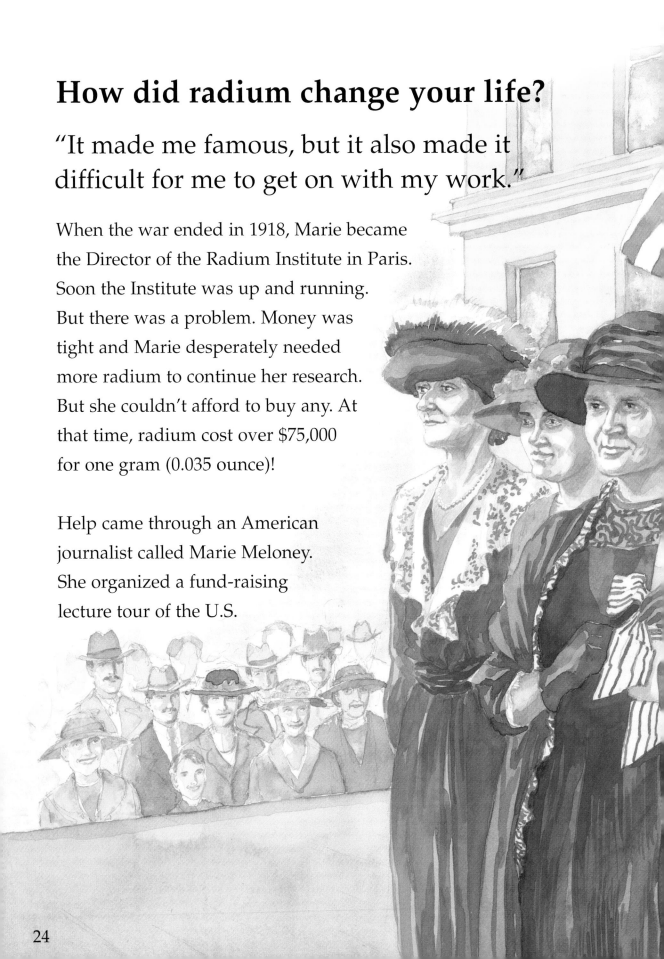

How did radium change your life?

"It made me famous, but it also made it difficult for me to get on with my work."

When the war ended in 1918, Marie became the Director of the Radium Institute in Paris. Soon the Institute was up and running. But there was a problem. Money was tight and Marie desperately needed more radium to continue her research. But she couldn't afford to buy any. At that time, radium cost over $75,000 for one gram (0.035 ounce)!

Help came through an American journalist called Marie Meloney. She organized a fund-raising lecture tour of the U.S.

The tour was a great success. Cheering crowds greeted Marie wherever she went. And in May, 1921, the President of the U.S. presented her with a gram (0.035 ounce) of radium.

Marie was a private person and she found fame very difficult to handle. It stopped her getting on with her work. She was also frequently ill. Today, people who work with radiation wear special protective clothing. But in Marie's day, nobody realized how dangerous it could be. Marie had worked with radiation every day for almost 25 years, with no protection at all.

How is Marie remembered today?

Marie continued to oversee the work of the Radium Institute in Paris, but her health grew steadily worse. She often felt dizzy and weak, as if she had a bad case of the flu, and had a painful humming in her ears. She could hardly see despite several operations on her eyes. Early on July 4, 1934 Marie Curie died of radiation sickness.

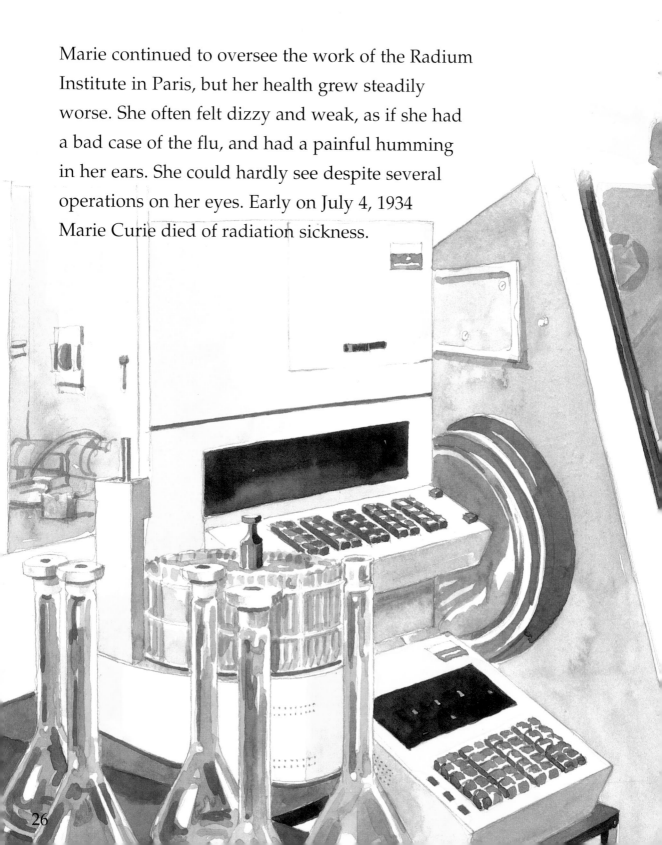

At the time of her death, Marie Curie was one of the most famous scientists in the world, and the first famous female scientist. Her daughter, Irène, followed in her footsteps. In 1935, she and her husband, Frédéric Joliot, won the Nobel Prize for Chemistry for their discovery of artificial radioactivity.

Marie's work lives on today. It helped scientists to learn much more about physics, especially about atoms and radioactivity. Today, radioactivity is used to run nuclear power stations, submarines, and in industry. It is also used in medical treatments. Thanks to Marie's research, scientists are finding out more about it all the time, both its uses and its dangers.

Some important dates

1859 Pierre Curie is born in France.

1867 Maria Salomee Sklodowska is born in Warsaw, Poland, on November 7.

1876 Marie's sisters Sofia and Bronya suffer from typhoid. Sofia dies in January, aged 13.

1878 Marie's mother dies of tuberculosis.

1883 Marie graduates from high school with distinction and wins a gold medal. She spends a year resting in the country.

1886–9 Marie leaves Warsaw and starts work as a governess in the country. She also teaches some local children. In her spare time, she studies physics and math.

1891 Marie leaves for Paris to study at the Sorbonne University.

1893 Marie receives her physics degree, with distinction.

1894 Marie receives a second degree in math. She meets Pierre Curie at the house of a friend.

1896 Marie marries Pierre Curie on July 26.

1897 Marie and Pierre's daughter, Irène, is born. Marie begins work on her research paper for her Doctor of Science.

1898 Marie and Pierre discover two new chemicals—polonium and radium.

1902 After four years' hard work, Marie finally makes a sample of pure radium and proves that it exists.

1903 Marie receives her Doctor of Science award. Marie, Pierre and Henri Becquerel share the Nobel Prize for Physics.

1904 Marie and Pierre's second daughter, Eve, is born. Pierre is appointed professor at the Sorbonne.

1906 Pierre is killed in a road accident. Marie becomes the first woman to give a lecture at the Sorbonne.

1911 Marie wins a second Nobel Prize for Chemistry.

1914 The Radium Institute is set up in Paris.

1914-18 The First World War. During the war, Marie organizes mobile X-ray units and trains 150 operators.

1921 Marie travels to the U.S. President Harding gives her one gram (0.035 ounce) of radium.

1926 Irène Curie marries French scientist, Frédéric Joliot.

1929 Marie's second visit to the U.S. President Hoover presents her with a gram (0.035 ounce) of radium for the Polish Radium Institute.

1934 On July 4, Marie dies of radiation poisoning. She is buried next to Pierre.

1935 Irène and Frédéric Joliot receive the Nobel Prize for Chemistry for their discovery of artificial radioactivity.

1995 Marie and Pierre's remains are moved to the Pantheon in Paris, watched by the French and Polish presidents.

Glossary

acid A chemical. Strong acids, such as sulfuric and nitric acids, are very dangerous because they can burn.

atoms Everything that exists is made up of atoms, the smallest things that can exist.

chemical A substance that is found in solid, liquid, or gas form. It changes when it is mixed with another chemical.

chemistry The study of chemicals and how they behave.

First World War The First World War broke out in 1914 between the Allies (Britain, France, Russia, and, in 1917, the U.S.) on one side, and the Central Powers (Germany, Austria-Hungary, and Turkey) on the other. The Allies were victorious.

governess A girl or woman employed in a private household to teach children.

graduate To pass your tests at a school or college and be awarded a certificate or a degree.

laboratory A room or building used by a scientist for carrying out experiments or research.

Nobel Prize One of the prizes awarded every year for outstanding work in physics and chemistry. There are also Nobel Prizes for medicine, literature, and for world peace. The prizes were set up by Alfred Nobel, the Swedish chemist and inventor, who died in 1896.

nuclear power Power produced when atoms are split apart. This gives off a huge amount of energy. In a nuclear power station, this energy is used to make electricity.

physics The study of how the universe works and how and why things happen in it. Physicists are scientists who study physics.

pitchblende A dark shiny rock that contains uranium and radium.

polonium A new radioactive substance found in pitchblende by Marie Curie in 1898.

radiation The names given to the rays that are given off when atoms break apart. Radiation can be very dangerous, causing burns and sickness. It can also be used to treat diseases such as cancer.

radiation sickness An illness caused by the effect of radiation on the body.

radioactivity The way in which rays are given off when atoms break apart. It is the way in which radiation is given off.

radium A brand-new substance discovered by Marie Curie in 1898.

rays Invisible rays of energy given off by certain substances. They include radiation, light waves, and X-rays.

tuberculosis A disease that affects a person's lungs. It also causes fever, weakness, weight loss, and severe coughing. It used to be known as consumption.

uranium A metal found in pitchblende that gives off radiation. It can be used to produce nuclear power.

X-rays A type of rays that can pass through soft materials, but not through solid material. This means that they can be used in hospitals—for example, to look at broken bones. They are also used at airports for checking baggage for dangerous objects.

Index

acid 19, 30
artificial radioactivity 27, 29
atoms 4, 17, 27, 30
Ayrton, Hertha 22

Becquerel, Henri 15, 20, 28

cancer 4, 22
chemicals 16-17, 18, 30
Curie, Irène 23, 27–29
Curie, Pierre 14, 18, 20, 28–29

First World War 23, 28, 30

Joliot, Frédéric 27–29

"Little Curies" 23

Marie's childhood 6–7
Marie's family 6–7, 10, 12, 28
Marie's health 250–27, 31
Marie's marriage 14
Marie's qualifications, 9, 13, 14,
  20, 28
Marie's schooldays 8-9
Meloney, Marie 24

Nobel prizes, 5, 20, 27– 29
Nobel prize for chemistry 20,
  27–29
Nobel prize for physics 20, 28
nuclear power 4, 27, 30

Paris 10, 12, 14, 20, 22, 26, 28
Pasteur Institute 22
physics 13, 27–28, 30–31
pitchblende 17–19, 31
Poland 6, 28–29
polonium 17, 28, 31

radiation 17, 22, 25–26, 29, 31
radioactivity 4, 22, 27, 31
radium 4, 17–19, 24–25, 28, 31
Radium Institute 22, 24, 26, 28
rays 4, 15, 31
Röntgen, Wilhelm 15

School of Physics 14, 16, 18
Sorbonne 10, 12–13, 20, 28–29

tuberculosis 7, 31
typhoid 28

uranium 15, 17, 31
U.S. 25, 28

Warsaw 6, 10, 28
women scientists 5, 27

X-rays 15, 23, 28, 31